More Energizing
Brain Breaks

Scott Mi

CORWIN

FOR INFORMATION:

Corwin
A SAGE Company
2455 Teller Road
Thousand Oaks, California 91320
(800) 233-9936
www.corwin.com

SAGE Publications Ltd.
1 Oliver's Yard
55 City Road
London EC1Y 1SP
United Kingdom

SAGE Publications India Pvt. Ltd.
B 1/I 1 Mohan Cooperative Industrial Area
Mathura Road, New Delhi 110 044
India

SAGE Publications Asia-Pacific Pte. Ltd.
18 Cross Street #10-10/11/12
China Square Central
Singapore 048423

Program Director: Jessica Allan
Cover Designer: Scott Van Atta
Typesetter: C&M Digitals (P) Ltd.

Printed in Canada

ISBN 978-1-5443-9908-9

This book is printed on acid-free paper.

19 20 21 22 23 10 9 8 7 6 5 4 3 2 1

About the Author

Scott Miller is currently a mathematics department chair in the Chicago area, where he collaborates with 26 math teachers in a school of 3,000 students. With more than 25 years of teaching experience, Scott has been instrumental as a K–12 project leader in mathematics curriculum and technology development. He has provided professional learning to thousands of educators on curriculum, assessment, technology, and the impact of movement and learning. Along with *More Energizing Brain Breaks*, he has co-authored innovative digital textbooks for Algebra 1, Geometry, and Algebra 2 and *Easy SMARTBoard Teaching Templates* with David Sladkey.

Welcome to *More Energizing Brain Breaks*

This book is a companion to Dave Sladkey's popular *Energizing Brain Breaks*. Brain Breaks are quick 1- to 2-minute activities which will help you and/or your audiences become re-focused and re-energized. They are like hitting your very own refresh button. Each of the 50 new activities will challenge your brain and get your body moving. *More Energizing Brain Breaks* can be used at home, in the office, in a classroom or during a meeting. They can be used in almost any setting. For instance, a teacher could have his or her class participate in a Brain Break to refocus students in the lesson. They can be used by anyone giving a presentation to help re-energize their audience. You can also take a Brain Break at the office to improve your productivity level.

This book includes 16 Brain Breaks that can be done individually. There are 24 partner **Brain Breaks** that are done with another person and include both competitive and non-competitive activities. There are 10 group Brain Break activities that promote team building.

individual

partner

group

This book also includes Re-engagement Strategies to help you, your class, or your group transition and re-focus after participating in a Brain Break. As a high school math teacher, I try to use an Energizing Brain Break followed by a re-engagement strategy every 25 minutes during classes.

Do you find yourself, your students, or your colleagues yawning and having a hard time staying focused during a meeting or a class?

More Energizing Brain Breaks is here to help! Just take a few minutes and try implementing a **Brain Break**. You, your colleagues, and/or your students will soon be refreshed, re-focused, re-energized, and re-engaged.

If you have ideas, comments or feedback you would like to share, I would love to hear from you at smhawkeye@gmail.com.

Kind regards,

Scott Miller

CROSSING THE MIDLINE

Most of the Brain Breaks involve cross-lateral movement. For example, when your right leg crosses over your left leg it is crossing the midline. This movement engages both hemispheres of the brain and promotes neural pathways between them.

All of the Brain Breaks involve some type of movement. The movement could be as simple as standing and balancing. Getting your body moving after sitting for a long period of time is refreshing. Movement during a Brain Break gives you a sense of renewed energy. Implement one today and you will experience the benefits.

The Crossover Brain Break
Promotes Movement and
Crosses the Midline

GETTING STARTED

1. OK, I've got the book and I'm ready to implement a Brain Break. What do I do next?

2. Select the number of people needed to demonstrate the Brain Break to come to the front of the room.

One person for an **individual**

Two persons for a **partner**

Three or more persons for a **group**

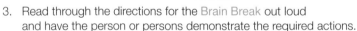

3. Read through the directions for the Brain Break out loud and have the person or persons demonstrate the required actions.

4. Have the rest of the people in the room perform the Brain Break.

More Energizing Brain Breaks

Ankle Touch

You will be touching your ankles using different patterns.

1. Stand up.

2. Spread your arms out.

3. Lift your right foot in front of you and touch your right ankle with your left hand. Put your right foot down.

4. Lift your left foot in front of you and touch your left ankle with your right hand. Put your left foot down.

5. Repeat steps 2 through 4 ten times.

6. Repeat steps 2 through 4 ten times but touch the bottom of your foot after touching your ankle.

Balancing on one leg is good for core strength.

Ankle Touch **Backwards**

You will be touching your ankle behind you using different patterns.

1. Stand up.

2. Spread your arms out.

3. Bend your left knee and lift your left foot behind you. Touch your left ankle with your right hand. Put your left foot down.

4. Bend your right knee and lift your right foot behind you. Touch your right ankle with your left hand. Put your right foot down.

5. Repeat steps 2 through 4 ten times.

6. Repeat steps 2 through 4 ten times but touch the bottom of your foot after touching your ankle.

Balancing on one leg is good for core strength.

Arm Reach

You will be reaching each arm in different directions.

1. Stand up.
2. Touch your hands to your shoulders.
3. Raise both hands above your head.
4. Touch your hands to your shoulders.
5. Extend your right arm out to the side while lowering your left arm to your side.
6. Touch your hands to your shoulders.
7. Lower your right arm to your side while raising your left arm above your head.
8. Touch your hands to your shoulders.
9. Extend your right arm to the side while lowering your left arm to your side.
10. Repeat steps 2 through 9 as fast as you can.
11. Switch right and left arms.

Idea from Kari Miller and Shelley Harmison Weeks

Calf Lift

You will be rising up on the tips of your toes.

1. Stand up with your feet shoulder-width apart.

2. Raise up on the toes of both feet 10 times.

3. Balance on your right foot and raise up on your right toes once.

4. Balance on your left foot and raise up on your left toes once.

5. Repeat steps 3 and 4 but increase the number of toe raises up to 10 on each foot. Then decrease the number of toe raises back down to one on each foot.

6. Repeat step 2 with your legs crossed.

Crossover

This activity requires you to cross the midline and maintain balance.

1. Stand up with your feet shoulder-width apart.

2. Hold your left earlobe with your right thumb and index finger.

3. Hold your right earlobe with your left thumb and index finger.

4. Inhale as you bend your knees and squat down.

5. Exhale as you stand back up. Repeat squatting and standing ten times.

6. Switch crossing your right arm over left arm and repeat steps 4 and 5.

7. To make the activity more challenging, cross your right leg over your left leg.

Elbow to Knee Switch

This stretching activity requires you to touch your elbow to your knee while sitting down.

1. Stand up and stretch your legs.
2. Sit down and cross your right leg over your left leg.
3. Place your left elbow on your right knee and grab your right earlobe with your left hand.
4. Switch and cross your left leg over your right leg. Place your right elbow on your left knee and grab your left earlobe with your right hand.
5. Switch back and forth as quickly as possible.

Crossing the midline engages both hemispheres of your brain.

Finger Aerobics **Lacing**

You will be making patterns with your fingers on each hand and switching.

1. Stand up.

2. Hold hands up, facing each other, with your fingers pointing straight up to the ceiling and your finger tips touching.

3. Place your right pinkie under your left pinkie. Your left pinkie should be resting over of your right pinkie.

4. Continue the process with placing your right ring finger over your left ring finger, your right middle finger under your left middle finger, your right index finger over your left index finger, and your right thumb under your left thumb.

5. Switch the lacing pattern so that right fingers that were over left fingers are now under left fingers and right fingers that were under left fingers are now over left fingers.

6. Repeat switching the lacing of your fingers as fast as possible.

Finger Aerobics **Spock**

You will be displaying an alternating pattern with your fingers on each hand and switching.

1. Stand up.

2. Hold up your hands in front of you, with your palms facing forward and fingers pointing straight up toward the ceiling.

3. On your right hand move your ring finger next to your pinkie and your middle finger next to your index finger. (Spock)

4. On your left hand move your ring finger and middle finger together. (Non-Spock)

5. Switch finger positions between both hands at the same time, so your left hand looks like your right hand and your right hand looks like your left hand.

6. Repeat switching your finger positions on each hand as fast as possible.

7. Try switching finger positions with your arms crossed, right over left or left over right.

I'm OK

You will be alternating a thumb toward yourself and an OK sign.

1. Stand up.

2. Point your right thumb toward your chest with your other right fingers curled up.

3. With your left hand make an OK sign. (Thumb and index finger tips touching, making an "O" shape, with other fingers pointing up.)

4. Switch and point your left thumb toward your chest and make an OK sign with your right hand.

5. Keep switching back and forth as fast as you can.

I'm OK, You're OK

You will be alternating a thumb toward yourself, the OK sign, and pointing.

1. Stand up.

2. Point your right thumb toward your chest with your other right fingers curled up. At the same time make an OK sign with your left hand.

3. Point your left index finger away from you and at the same time make the OK sign with your right hand.

4. Repeat steps 2 and 3 ten times as fast as possible.

5. Switch hands and repeat steps 2 and 3 ten times as fast as possible.

Itsy Bitsy Spider

**You know the old rhyme that says
"The itsy bitsy spider went up the water spout . . .**

1. Stand up.
2. Put your hands out in front of you.
3. Take your left thumb and touch it to your right index finger.
4. Take your left index finger and touch it to your right thumb.

5. While pivoting on your left index finger and right thumb, rotate both hands upward so that you can now reach your left thumb to your right index finger. Continue rotating your fingers and thumbs upward so that they are "walking up the water spout."
6. Repeat the process behind your back.
7. Repeat going "down the water spout."
8. Once you've mastered this, perform the same process with your index fingers and your pinkies.

Idea from Dave Sladkey

Jump Square

You will be crossing your feet while jumping in an alternating pattern.

1. Stand up with your feet shoulder-width apart.

2. Jump and land with your right foot crossed over in front your left foot.

3. Jump and land with your feet uncrossed shoulder-width apart.

4. Jump and land with your left foot crossed over in front of your right foot.

5. Jump and land with your feet uncrossed.

6. Jump and land with your right foot crossed over in front of your left foot and then jump and switch quickly so that your left foot crosses over in front of your right foot.

7. Jump and land with your feet uncrossed.

8. Repeat steps 2 through 7 fast as you can.

Paper Toss

You will be throwing a ball of paper over your shoulder.

1. Stand up and find a sheet of scrap paper.
2. Crumple up the paper into a ball.
3. Place the ball into your left hand and move your left hand behind your back.
4. Toss the ball forward over your right shoulder and catch it with your right hand.
5. Repeat for 20 seconds.
6. Switch so that the ball is in your right hand and you toss the ball over your left shoulder.
7. Repeat for 20 seconds.
8. To add difficulty to the activity, try to toss and catch with the same hand.

This activity is good for improving hand-eye coordination.

Snap Wink

This activity requires you to switch snapping and winking.

1. Stand up.
2. Wink your left eye and snap your right hand index finger and thumb at the same time.
3. Wink your right eye and snap your left hand index finger and thumb at the same time.
4. Switch back and forth as fast as you can.

Engaging both hemispheres of the brain promotes neural pathways.

Standing Balance

This activity requires you to maintain your balance.

1. Stand up.
2. Extend both arms out to your sides and balance on your left foot for 10 seconds.
3. Keep arms extended and balance on your right foot for 10 seconds
4. With arms extended, tilt your head back and touch your nose with alternating right and left index fingers five times each while balancing on your left foot.
5. Repeat step 4 while balancing on your right foot.
6. Repeat steps 2 through 5 with your eyes closed.

Balancing on one leg is good for core strength.

15

Waiter/Waitress

You will be balancing and rotating a folder without dropping it.

1. Stand up.

2. Rest a folder or notebook on the palm of your right hand in front of you, like a waiter or waitress holding a tray.

3. While balancing the folder or notebook on your hand, maneuver it so that the folder or notebook is now behind you, still balanced on your right palm.

4. Flair your arm out away from you. Again, keep the folder or notebook balanced on the palm of your right hand.

5. Continue rotating your arm so that the folder or notebook will return to the starting position in front of you.

6. After mastering this with your right hand, repeat steps 2 through 5 with your left hand.

Idea from Randy Smith

Animal Fist Bump 1

You will make different animal shapes using your hands.

1. Stand up, find a partner, and face each other.

2. Decide who is Person A and who is Person B.

3. Person A makes a fist with his/her right hand. Person B makes a fist with his/her left hand.

4. As the partners move their fists toward each other to do a fist bump, Person A says either the word "snail" or "narwhal."

5. If Person A says "snail" then Person B sticks out the index and middle fingers (like snail antennae) on his/her left hand and moves these two fingers below the fist of Person A while bumping knuckles with Person A's fist.

6. If Person A says "narwhal" then Person B sticks out the index finger (like a narwhal tooth) on his/her left hand and moves this finger above the fist of Person A while bumping knuckles with Person A's fist. Do this as fast as you can.

7. Once Person A has led for a while, switch and have Person B lead.

8. Use two hands to add difficulty to the activity.

Idea from Erica Conway and Kara Wojcik

partner

Animal Fist Bump 2

You will make different animal shapes using your hands.

1. Stand up, find a partner, and face each other.
2. Decide who is Person A and who is Person B.
3. Person A makes a fist with his/her left or right hand. Person B makes fists with both hands.

Moose

4. As the partners move their fists towards each other to do a fist bump, Person A says either the word "moose" or "peacock."
5. If Person A says "moose" then Person B places both hands with fingers outstretched on either side of Person A's fist (like moose antlers) with thumbs touching the fist.
6. If Person A says "peacock" then Person B flips both hands around and places both hands next to each other, with backsides against Person A's fist (like peacock feathers).

Peacock

7. Do this as fast as you can. Once person A has led for a while, switch and have person B lead.

Animal Five

You will make different animal shapes using your hands.

1. Stand up, find a partner, and face each other.

2. Decide who is Person A and who is Person B.

3. Person A holds up his/her right hand fingers up, palm side toward Person B. Person B holds up his/her left hand in the same manner, palm side toward Person A.

4. As the partners move their hands toward each other as to do a high five, Person A says either "turkey" or "jellyfish."

5. If Person A says "turkey" then Person B makes a thumbs up with his/her left hand and places the pinkie end (base) of his/her fist onto the high five of Person A.

6. If Person A says "jellyfish" then both Person A and Person B make "jellyfish" with their own hand. They touch their own fingertips and thumb together, then separate their finger, then touch, then separate. They repeat this action while moving their hands away from each other.

7. Do this as fast as you can. Once Person A has led for a while, switch and have Person B lead.

8. Use two hands to add difficulty to the activity.

Idea from Erica Conway and Kara Wojcik

19

Clocked

You will make time on a clock that adds to 12 o'clock.

1. Stand up, find a partner, and face each other.

2. Decide who is Person A and who is Person B.

3. Person A will select an hour other than 12 o'clock.

4. Person A will extend his/her arms around him/herself, like the "hands" of a clock, to depict the hour he/she has selected. The minute arm will be fully extended toward 12 o'clock. The hour arm will be drawn in a bit, bent at the elbow with the hand pointing toward the hour. At the same time Person A says the hour that he/she has selected and is depicting. (Note that Person A's arms must display the time so that it is readable to Person B).

Two o' clock

5. Person B will mentally calculate what "hour" must be added to Person A's hour so that they add up to 12. Person B will then use his/her arms (as in step 4) to depict the hour while he/she says the hour that was calculated and being shown. (For example, if Person A depicts and says, "Two o'clock," then Person B must depict and say, "Ten o'clock.")

6. Switch so that Person B selects and depicts the "hour" first and Person A makes the corresponding "hour" that will add to 12 o'clock.

7. Repeat as fast as possible.

To increase difficulty, include times at 15, 30, or 45 minutes past the hour.

Finger Aerobics

You will copy finger movements of your partner.

1. Find a partner and sit across from each other at a desk or table.

2. Place both hands on the desk or table.

3. Person A begins by lifting one finger and putting it back down. Person B copies the movement by lifting the finger directly across from Person A's finger (like a mirror image).

4. Person A continues by lifting the same finger in step 3, putting it down, and then lifting a different finger and putting it down. Person B copies the two finger pattern.

5. Continue this routine with Person A adding a different finger lift to the prior pattern and Person B copying the new pattern until a pattern of 10 finger lifts have been made and copied.

6. Switch so that Person B is the leader and Person A copies the finger lifting patterns.

To increase the difficulty, choose a pattern that uses two fingers.

Fist and Five

You will alternate high five and fist bumps with your partner.

1. Stand up.
2. Find a partner and face each other.
3. Each person makes a fist with his/her right hand (fingers down) and a "high five" with their left hand (palm forward, fingers extended up and together). Each person makes their fist bump into the palm of his/her partner's "high five."

4. Each person switches his/her right hand to a "high five" and his/her left hand to a fist and each makes their fist bump into the other's "high five."
5. Each person switches his/her right hand to a fist and his/her left hand to a "flip high five." (A "flip high five" is a "high five" with the hand turned around so the back of the hand faces forward). Each fist bumps the other's "flip high five."
6. Each person switches his/her right hand to a "flip high five" and his/her left hand to a fist. Each fist bumps the other's "flip high five."
7. Repeat steps 3 through 6 as fast as possible.
8. Repeat with arms crossed.

Idea from Tony Schlorff

Hand Shake

You will be performing a lengthy hand shake with your partner.

1. Stand up, find a partner, and face each other.
2. Person A slaps down-facing open right hand on Person B's up-facing open right hand. Then Person B does the same to Person A.
3. Each person turns their right hands sideways and slaps palm sides together and then the backs of their right hands together.
4. The partners shake right hands and then shift their grasp upward so that each person holds the thumb of his/her partner and points index fingers at each other.
5. Each partner releases, slides hand back slightly and touches right thumbs. With right thumbs touching, each partner curls the other fingers in and pivots right hands around each other so that the backs of the right hands are touching and fingers are extended.
6. The partners flip right hands down so right palms are touching and hook right thumbs.
7. With thumbs hooked, twist hands around so that both palms face down, making the wings of a bird.
8. Each partner flaps their wing of the bird and moves his/her hand upward while keeping the thumbs hooked.
9. Repeat this hand shake with your left hand.
10. Finally try the hand shake with both hands at the same time.

partner

You will be shaking the ankle of your partner in this handshake.

1. Stand up and find a partner.
2. Face your partner so that your right shoulders are across from each other.
3. Shake right hands.
4. Touch right elbows twice.
5. Do two right hand fist bumps. (A fist bump is making a fist and lightly bumping the upper fingers and knuckles.)
6. Do two right hand hammer taps each. (A hammer tap is making a fist and tapping the bottom of one person's fist to the top of another person's fist.)
7. Tap the insides of the right feet twice.
8. Tap the outsides of the right feet twice.
9. While standing on your left foot, lean forward with your right hand and arm extended and lift your right foot up behind you. Grasp your partner's right ankle and shake lightly twice.
10. Let go and stand up.
11. Slide so that your left shoulders are across from each other.
12. Repeat the process with left hands and left feet.

Mirror Moves

You will be mirroring your partner's moves.

1. Stand up, find a partner, and face each other.

2. Decide who is Person A and who is Person B.

3. Person A moves his/her right hand while Person B mirrors the movement with his/her left hand.

4. Person A continues moving his/her right hand and then begins moving his/her left foot. Person B mirrors the movements with his/her left hand and right foot.

5. Switch hands and feet, with Person A continuing to lead.

6. Switch so that Person B leads and Person A mirrors the movements.

Balancing on one leg is good for core strength.

More Moves - Rotation

You will make a 180° rotation of your partner's moves.

1. Stand up, find a partner, and face each other.

2. Decide who is Person A and who is Person B.

3. Person A moves his/her right hand while Person B copies the movement with his/her right hand.

4. Person A continues moving his/her right hand and then begins moving his/her right foot. Person B copies the movements with his/her right hand and right foot.

5. Switch hands and feet, with Person A continuing to lead.

6. Switch so that Person B leads and Person A leads the movement.

Balancing on one leg is good for core strength.

Quick Math **Addition**

You and your partner will each reveal a certain number of fingers to each other. The first person to add them together first wins the round.

1. Stand up and find a partner. A group of three works as well.

2. Face your partner and put both hands behind your back.

3. Each person chooses from one to ten fingers with his/her hands.

4. Both persons say, "One, two, three QUICKMATH." When the word "QUICKMATH" is said, each person moves his/her hands in front of him/herself at the same time displaying their chosen number with their fingers.

5. The person who adds the numbers together and says the total correctly first is the winner of that round.

6. Play the best of five rounds.

Idea from Jean Blaydes

Quick Math **Multiplication**

You and your partner will each reveal a certain number of fingers to each other. The first person to multiply them together first wins the round.

1. Stand up and find a partner. A group of three works as well.

2. Face your partner and put both hands behind your back.

3. Each person chooses from one to ten fingers with his/her hands.

4. Both persons will say, "One, two, three QUICKMATH." When the word "QUICKMATH" is said, each person moves his/her hands in front of him/herself at the same time displaying their chosen number with their fingers.

5. The person who multiplies the numbers together and says the total correctly first is the winner of that round.

6. Play the best of five rounds.

Quick Math **Negative**

You and your partner will each reveal a certain number of fingers to each other. The first person to add them together first wins the round.

1. Stand up and find a partner. A group of three works as well. Choose one person to represent negative numbers.

2. Face your partner and put both hands behind your back.

3. Each person chooses from one to ten fingers with his/her hands.

4. Both persons will say, "One, two, three QUICKMATH." When the word "QUICKMATH" is said, each person moves his/her hands in front of him/herself at the same time displaying their chosen number with their fingers.

5. The person who adds the negative number with the positive number together and says the total correctly first is the winner of that round.

6. Play the best of five rounds.

partner

Rock, Paper, Scissors

This activity is a twist on the traditional game.

1. Stand up, find a partner, and face each other.

2. Decide who is Person A and who is Person B.

3. Both partners place their right hand behind their back.

4. Person A will make Rock, Paper, or Scissors with his/her right hand and then will move his/her hand selection to the front for Person B to see.

5. Person B will now make Rock, Paper, or Scissors with his/her right and move his/her right hand to the front as quickly as possible in order to beat Person A. (Remember Rock beats Scissors, Paper beats Rock, and Scissors beats Paper.)

6. Repeat this five times with Person B beating Person A.

7. Switch with Person A beating Person B.

Idea from Paul Zientarski

Rock, Paper, Scissors **Lose**

You are trying to lose to your partner in the traditional game with a twist.

1. Stand up, find a partner, and face each other.

2. Decide who is Person A and who is Person B.

3. Both partners place their right hand behind their back.

4. Person A will make Rock, Paper, or Scissors with his/her right hand and then will move his/her hand selection to the front for Person B to see.

5. Person B will now make Rock, Paper, or Scissors with his/her right and move his/her right hand to the front as quickly as possible in order to lose to Person A. (Remember Rock loses to Paper, Paper loses to Scissors, and Scissors loses to Rock.)

6. Repeat this five times with Person B losing to Person A.

7. Switch with Person A losing to Person B.

partner

Rock, Paper, Scissors **Doubled**

This activity is a twist on the traditional game using two hands.

1. Stand up, find a partner, and face each other.

2. Decide who is Person A and who is Person B.

3. Both partners place their hands behind their backs.

4. Person A will make Rock, Paper, or Scissors with his/her right and left hands. They can be the same or different. Then Person A will move his/her selections to the front for Person B to see.

5. Person B will now make Rock, Paper, or Scissors with his/her hands and move his/her hands to the front as quickly as possible in order to beat Person A's right hand and lose to Person A's left hand. (Remember Rock beats Scissors, Paper beats Rock, and Scissors beats Paper.)

6. Repeat this five times with Person A beginning.

7. Switch with Person B beginning.

Say Z and Win

You and your partner are trying to be the person to say the letter Z by going through the alphabet.

1. Stand up, find a partner, and face each other.

2. Decide who is Person A and who is Person B.

3. Person A chooses a letter from "A" to "E" to start the game. Person A can say that letter only or that letter and the next letter in the alphabet.

4. Person B then says the next letter or the next two letters in the alphabet. Each person takes turns saying either one or two letters at a time. For example, if Person A just took his/her turn and said the letter "E", then Person B could say either "F" or "F" and "G."

5. The alternating turns continue through the alphabet until the winner says the letter "Z."

6. Play the game again with Person B choosing the starting letter.

Idea from Sam Sterling

partner

Slap Letter

Partners alternate slapping each other's hands while saying letters.

1. Stand up, find a partner, and face each other.

2. Decide who is Person A and who is Person B.

3. Face your partner with your hands forward and palms up.

4. Person A: Take your right hand and cross over and slap Person B's right hand lightly and say the letter "A." Now take your left hand and cross over and slap Person B's left hand and say the letter "B."

5. Person B: Repeat the actions of Person A but say the letters "C" and "D."

6. The alternating turns continue until the letter "Z" is said.

7. For the next round, begin with the letter Z and slap letters going backwards by every other letter. (Z, X, V . . .)

Try going backwards or forwards by three or four letters at a time.

Slap Letter, Say Z, and Win

You and your partner are trying to be the person to say the letter Z by going through the alphabet and using Slap Letter at the same time.

1. Stand up, find a partner, and face each other.

2. Decide who is Person A and who is Person B.

3. Face your partner with your hands forward and palms up.

4. Person A chooses a letter from "A" to "E" to start the game. Person A can say that letter only or that letter and the next letter in the alphabet while at the same time performing Slap Letter. Person A takes his/her right hand, crosses over and slaps Person B's right hand lightly while saying a letter. If desired, Person A takes his/her left hand, crosses over and slaps Person B's left hand lightly while saying the next letter in the alphabet.

5. Person B then says the next letter or the next two letters in the alphabet while performing Slap Letter also. Each person takes turns saying and slapping either one or two letters at a time. For example, if Person A just took his/her turn and said and slapped the letter "E", then Person B could say and slap either "F" or "F" and "G."

6. The alternating turns continue through the alphabet until the winner says and slaps the letter "Z."

7. Play the game again with Person B choosing the starting letter.

Tap Count

Partners alternate tapping each other's feet while saying numbers.

1. Stand up, find a partner, and face each other.

2. Decide who is Person A and who is Person B.

3. Person A: Move your right foot forward and tap the inside of Person B's right foot and say the number "1." With your left foot, tap the inside of Person B's left foot and say the number "2."

4. Person B: Repeat the actions of Person A but say the numbers "3" and "4."

5. The alternating turns continue until the you have tap counted up to the number "40."

6. For the next round, begin with the number "34" and tap count down by 3's.

Try going up or down by any number.

Third Base Coach **Letters**

Without talking, you will be pointing to spots on yourself like a third base coach, and then your partner will "read" the letters to determine what the word is.

1. Stand up and find a partner. Decide who is Person A and who is Person B.

2. Take a few moments to think of a word that involves the letters A, B, C, D, E, F, G, H, I and J.

3. The letter spots are: right wrist = A, right elbow = B, right shoulder = C, right ear = D, nose = E, left ear = F, left shoulder = G, left elbow = H, left wrist = I, and abdomen = J.

Letter B

4. Without talking, Person A spells a word by touching letter spots on him/herself. Person B says each of the letters out loud and says the word that was spelled. For example, Person A might touch his/her left elbow, then his/her nose. Person B would say "H . . . E . . . he."

5. Switch and have Person B spell a word.

Try two letter words to start with and work up to longer words.

Third Base Coach Addition

**Without talking, you will be pointing to spots on yourself like a
third base coach, and then your partner will "read" the
numbers to determine what the sum is.**

1. Stand up and find a partner. Decide who is Person A and
   who is Person B.
2. The number spots are: right wrist = 1, right elbow = 2,
   right shoulder = 3, right ear = 4, nose = 5, left ear = 6,
   left shoulder = 7, left elbow = 8, left wrist = 9, and
   abdomen = 10.
3. Without talking, Person A touches two of the number
   spots on him/herself. Person B says each of the numbers
   out loud, adds them together, and says the sum. For
   example, Person A might touch his/her left shoulder and
   then his/her left wrist. Person B would say "seven plus nine
   equals sixteen."
4. Switch and have Person B give an addition problem.

Number 9

**Try two numbers to start with and work up to
adding three or four numbers at a time.**

Without talking, you will be pointing to spots on yourself like a third base coach, and then your partner will "read" the problem to determine what the product is.

1. Stand up and find a partner. Decide who is Person A and who is Person B.
2. The number spots are: right wrist = 1, right elbow = 2, right shoulder = 3, right ear = 4, nose = 5, left ear = 6, left shoulder = 7, left elbow = 8, left wrist = 9, and abdomen = 10.
3. Without talking, Person A touches two of the number spots on him/herself. Person B says each of the numbers out loud, multiplies them together, and says the product. For example, Person A might touch his/her right shoulder and then his/her left elbow. Person B would say "three times eight equals twenty four."
5. Switch and have Person B give a multiplication problem.

Try two numbers to start with and work up to three or four numbers at a time.

This is My Nose

This activity will stretch your mind to say one thing and do another.

1. Stand up, find a partner, and face each other.

2. Decide who is Person A and who is Person B.

3. Person A points to a part of his/her body, but calls it by another name. For example, Person A might point to his/her foot and say, "This is my nose."

4. Person B must answer in reverse. Using the above example, Person B would point to his/her nose and say, "This is my foot."

5. Continue with Person A leading nine more times, then switch to Person B leading.

"This is my nose."

Idea from Debra Adams

Action Punctuation

**This activity requires groups to make actions
and sounds for punctuation marks.**

1. Select a reading passage (fiction or nonfiction) and display it or make copies.
2. Divide into groups for each of the types of punctuation in the reading passage (period, quotation marks, question mark, exclamation point, comma, hyphen, etc.).
3. Assign a punctuation mark to each group.
4. Instruct each group to make up an action and a sound for their punctuation mark.

5. Have each group perform their punctuation mark, action, and sound.
6. The instructor then reads the reading passage out loud once to the class.
7. The instructor reads through the passage out loud a second time, during which each group will stand and perform their action and sound when the instructor comes to their punctuation mark. As the instructor, make sure to read slowly and pause for the action punctuation.

Idea from Marc O'Shea

41

Brain Drain

After learning a difficult concept, students will communicate their understanding to reinforce knowledge.

1. Stand up.

2. Walk five steps in any direction and find a partner.

3. Take turns explaining the difficult concept to each other for 30 seconds each.

4. When the time is up, walk five steps in a different direction and find a new partner.

5. Take turns telling each other what you heard about the difficult concept from your previous partner for 30 seconds each.

6. When time is called, return to your seat and "brain drain" by writing down your understanding of the difficult concept.

Repetition helps to reinforce learning.

Idea from Paul Zientarski

Groups will try to send the alternating current the fastest.

1. Divide into two groups. Have each group stand in a line on either side of the instructor and hold hands forming two chains of people.

2. The instructor holds the hand of the first person of each chain and lightly squeezes both hands at the same time starting an "alternating electric current" going down both chains of people.

3. The first person in each chain lightly squeezes the instructor's hand to change the direction of the "alternating current." Then the instructor lightly squeezes the first person's hand again to continue the "alternating current."

4. The first person in each chain lightly squeezes the second person's hand. Then the second person squeezes the first person's hand to change the direction of the "alternating electric current." The current is sent all the way back to the instructor.

5. The pattern repeats by adding another person to the alternating current until the last person in each chain taps a desk twice after receiving the "alternating electric current" and then returns the current up the chain.

6. The first group to send and receive the "alternating electric current" down their chain and up to the instructor the fastest is to winner.

7. Repeat with arms crossed.

Electricity DC

Groups will try to send the direct current the fastest.

1. Divide into two groups. Have each group stand in a line on either side of the instructor and hold hands forming two chains of people.

2. The instructor holds the hand of the first person of each chain and lightly squeezes both hands at the same time starting a "direct electric current" going down each chain of people.

3. Each person in the chain lightly squeezes the next person's hand after receiving the "direct current" from the previous person.

4. The person at the end of each chain taps a desk twice after receiving the "direct current" and then returns the current back up the chain.

5. The first group to send and receive the "direct current" through their chain and back to the instructor three times the fastest is the winner.

6. Repeat with arms crossed.

Gotcha Feet

Try to pin another person's foot, while at the same time avoid having your foot pinned by another person.

1. Stand up and divide into groups of 3 to 10 people.
2. Each group should form a circle.
3. Each person in each circle should place his/her left foot toes above the right foot toes of the person to his/her left. Each person should be standing on his/her right foot and resting on his/her left heel.

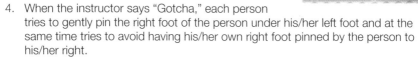

4. When the instructor says "Gotcha," each person tries to gently pin the right foot of the person under his/her left foot and at the same time tries to avoid having his/her own right foot pinned by the person to his/her right.
5. Repeat for several rounds
6. Switch with the right foot trying to pin left foot.

People should have close-toed shoes on to perform this activity.

Idea from John Fiore

Hand Jive

This activity uses repeated hand motions.

1. Stand up and face the front of the room.
2. Slap hands on thighs twice.
3. Clap hands twice.
4. With palms down and hands not touching, pass right hand over left hand twice. Then pass left hand over right hand twice.
5. Make fists with fingers and hammer tap right fist on top of left fist twice. Then hammer tap left fist on top of right fist twice. (A hammer tap is making a fist and tapping the bottom of one fist to the top of the other.)
6. Stick out thumb on right hand and point it back over the right shoulder twice. Stick out thumb on left hand and point it back over the left shoulder twice.
7. Continue repeating this pattern faster and faster.
8. Make your own pattern.

This is a great activity to do with music.

Human Knot

This activity requires groups to untangle the knot that they form.

1. Stand up and get into groups of 5 to 8 people.
2. Have each person join right hands with another person in their group that is not standing immediately to his/her left or right.
3. Then have each person in their group join left hands with another person in their group that is not standing immediately to his/her left or right. This cannot be the same person that he/she joined right hands with.
4. Now the groups have to work together to untangle the knot without letting go of their hands.
5. People may need to loosen their grip in order to twist and turn.
6. People may also have to step over or under each other.
7. The first group to untangle their knot is the winner.

This activity is good for group problem solving.

Line Up 1

This activity uses non-verbal communication to organize a group.

1. Stand up.

2. Instruct the group that they may not use verbal communication during this activity. (No talking!)

3. Tell the group that they must line up from youngest to oldest across the front of the room as quickly as possible. This includes the month, day, and year.

4. Remind the group that they must use other forms of communication such as hand gestures.

The group could also arrange themselves in their seats.

Idea from Paul Chelsen

Line Up 2

This activity uses non-verbal communication to organize a group.

1. Stand up. (No talking!)

2. Instruct the group that they may not use verbal communication during this activity.

3. Tell group that they must line up across the front of the room alphabetically by their names as quickly as possible. This includes first, middle, and last names.

5. Remind the group that they must use other forms of communication such as hand gestures.

6. Try having the group arrange themselves using their first or last name backwards.

The group could also arrange themselves in their seats.

Shape It Up

Groups will be making shapes using only their arms.

1. Stand up and divide into groups of 3 to 6 people.
2. Each group forms a circle.
3. Inform groups that they will be given a shape to make as a group using only their arms, from elbow to fingertip, as sides of the shape.
4. The instructor selects one of the following shapes and announces it to the groups: right triangle, isosceles triangle, equilateral triangle, square, rectangle, rhombus, parallelogram, pentagon, hexagon, octagon, five-pointed star, or six-pointed star.

parallelogram

5. Each group must make the shape using at least one arm from each person in the group.
6. Repeat steps 4 and 5 with another shape.

Persons in groups could also bend their wrists to make additional sides to the shape.

Re-engagement Strategies

**These strategies will help to focus people's attention
after performing a brain break.**

1. Tell people, "Let me see your eyes" several times until you have their attention.
2. Hold up a pen and say, "Look at the tip of this pen. What color is it?"
3. Approach a couple of people and say, "If you can hear my voice, clap your hands once." Continue with, "If you can hear my voice, clap your hands twice." Continue this until you have the entire groups' attention.
4. Use a timer so that the brain break has a time limit.
5. Tell people to turn around twice when they are finished with the brain break.
6. Tell people to sit down when they are finished with the activity.
7. Tell people to stand on their seats when they are finished with the brain break.
8. Use a bell or clicker to signal the end of an activity.
9. Use music to let students know to transition out of the brain break.
10. Stop the activity and have the group members write a quick response.

Eventually re-engaging people will become a routine.

Write Your Own Brain Break

Write Your Own Brain Break

ACKNOWLEDGMENTS

I would like to thank Jean Blaydes for inspiring me to integrate movement and learning.

I would like to thank Dr. John Ratey and Dr. John Medina for researching and writing about the brain and how exercise impacts how we learn.

Thank you to Paul Zientarski for his leadership on changing physical education from skill development into life-long fitness.

Thanks also go to David Sladkey for encouraging me to write this book and for his daily examples of how to use movement in the classroom.

Thank you to my colleagues in the Math Department at Naperville Central High School for their innovation and ideas as to how to engage students on a daily basis.

This book would not be possible without the help of my children, Kari, Kirsten, and Audrey. Their feedback and willingness to try brain break ideas were invaluable. Finally, I would like to thank my amazing wife, Laura, for her inspiration and for her assistance in editing this book.

Helping educators make the greatest impact

CORWIN HAS ONE MISSION: to enhance education through intentional professional learning.

We build long-term relationships with our authors, educators, clients, and associations who partner with us to develop and continuously improve the best evidence-based practices that establish and support lifelong learning.